Dark Poeta

Vega Starlight

No part of this book may be reproduced or transmitted in any form or by any means whatsoever without express written permission from Vega Starlight

ISBN 978-0-578-30830-2

Copyright © 2022 by Vega Starlight Publishing

All rights reserved

Email: starlightvega1@gmail.com
Instagram: vega_starlight_

Dedicated to those who:

judged, doubted, denied, insulted,
demeaned, insinuated, poked, prodded,
ignored, rejected, disassociated, lied,
spied, reprised, lamented, opined,
abandoned, criticized, pried, notified
tried, untried, uncodified,
slew, whew, shoo,
unaccompanied, misclassified,
oversimplified

This is for you.

Or perhaps this is not for you.

Let us not quibble over the details.

Also dedicated to those who:

Found themselves on the far side of the bridge.

Lift up your chin.
Lift up your eyes.
Dry your tears.
No more looking backwards.
Look at yourself.
Look inside.
Gaze into the mirror.
Ponder the future.
Take my hand.
Palaver with me.

We are together.

Contents

If, Then	14
Welcome!	15
Dark Poeta	19
Vega Starlight	27
The Door Test	32
Repent	36
Mirror Mirror	38
Good Days, Bad Days	42
Tiny Fish, Tiny Bowl	46
Trash	47
Sarah	49
Morning Star	53
Walking Away from Rainbows	54
Indifference	55
La Flaka	58
Sugar Pie	60
Carte Blanche	62
The Path Narrows	66
The Rankle and File	70
Twinkle, Twinkle	71
Black Orchid	73
Cancel Me	74
Cabin Fever	76
Blackbirds (Mind the Hawk)	79
Raine	80
Crazy People	81
Moth	82
The Tiniest Witch	86
Razor Blade Rituals	88
Persephone	90
After the Snow	98
Tiffany	101
Bleed Inside	102

Lex Rex	105
Forget	108
Queen	109
Reprobate	112
Don't You Want To…?	118
Venus	120
Winter Before Sunrise	124
Home	128
Billet-Doux	136
On Greatness	137
Crush	138
No Strings	141
Cold Bricks	143
Bijoux	144
Immortal	152
Cinderella	154
The Matador	155
Dichotomy	156
White Silence	160
Black Noise	163
Alone	164
Lilith	166
Why?	167
Prisoner	168
Lonely	169
Best Friend	172
Sophia	176
Blank Slate	182
Finish	186
The End	188

IF

You read this book.

IF

You find yourself feeling uncomfortable.

IF

You are overcome with thoughts of regret and remorse.

IF

You question every decision you have ever made.

IF

You find yourself HATING me.

THEN

I have done my job.

Ladies and Gentlemen,
Welcome one and all ^FREAK
To the greatest ~~show~~ on earth!

DARK POETA

^AKA   The Nocturnal Circus
^AKA   The Psycho Circus
^AKA   The One True Ringmaster

^AKA **VEGA STARLIGHT**

Are you ready to witness my mind?

LIAR

DARK POETA

Step right up and witness the breakup.
The breakdown of all rationality.
Ladies and gentlemen! Witness me.
The Ringmaster - your host, your guide, your therapy.

VEGA STARLIGHT

Tickets cost thirteen-ninty-nine.
An unmatched value - more potent than Valium!
Step right up and experience the fucked up.
Hold your gasps! (and orgasms!) This is just foreplay.

~~PANTIES~~ ~~SLIP~~

Pull the curtain to the side - step inside.
The circus is in town for a limited time!
Dark Poeta, the nocturnal circus.
The circus train comes and goes - ghosted.

Nocturnal insomniac. Carnivorous psychotic.
Ladies and gentlemen! Experience the exotic.
But leave your ~~children~~ MISTAKES at home.
I am trying to operate a reputable business here!

Take a seat and adjust your gaze.
Focus on me in the center ring.

> RING MY BELL
> WRING MY NECK
> WHIP ME, HURT ME
> I'M A WRECK

There is no quarter here.
No safe place - not for you nor for peers.
Nonsensical yet consequential fear.
Oh, I will jeer - your mascara will smear.

The longer the show, the deeper we go.
Voyeur, conspirator - guilty by association.
Clap your hands! One, two, three, ~~four~~.

> YOU FORGOT THE FOURTH BEATING

Beat me four times.
Rape me four times.
I am my own worst enemy.
But your worst enemy, too.

This Ringmaster.
This Coordinator.
This Instigator.
This sickening idea Generator.

What's wrong with me? **TELL ME**
Ladies and gentlemen, I implore you.
Come and see! What is wrong with me?
  YOU ARE WRONG WITH ME

Cough, cough. Excuse me please.
Through the crowd, I can not see!
A humble Ringmaster? **NARCISSIST**
Pity me. No, wait. Do not pity me.

The deeper I go,
The less you think.
The longer the show,
The further you sink.

Wallow with me.
Balls deep in the mud.
Smear lipstick on me.
Wrestle a pig.

  **INFECT ME
  WITH YOUR IMPURITY**

There is a game I play.
At the bottom of the well.
We live at the bottom.
Yes, we. People like YOU and me.

Because inside.
We.
Inside of you and me.
We are the same. FALSE

Ringmasters of the nothing.
The FECKLESS nothing.
We have nowhere.
Descend to the bottom of the well with me.

Lift your skirt.
Don't get wet.
Lift your skirt.
Show me your wet.

The longer the show,
The less sense you make.
Choking, gagging, drooling.
You make perfect sense!

WHERE IS THE EXIT?

Do you not yet see?
Between you and me.
There is no exit - leashed to me.
Permanently. YES, MY MASTER

The bottom is where I belong.
The wet is where you belong.

Suffer with me.

We have lost all control!
But only of the clowns.
Try this muzzle.
A perfect fit!

Ladies and gentlemen!

Please report to the nearest emergency exit.
BUT THE LEASH IS TAUT

Ladies and troglodytes.
Ladies and mouth-breathers.
Trash.
The disposable, the flushable.
BLOODY TAMPON

Fire! Fire! PANIC!

Sluts and rapists.
Tell me the difference.
Sashay yourself to the center ring.
Enlighten the audience of difference.

The taut leash.
The collar biting into porcelain flesh.
Dragging, kicking, screaming, runny mascara.
Clown paint.

All sluts report to the center ring!
BUT THERE IS A FIRE!

At the stake,
We burn the witch.
Except the pregnant,
Milk the bitch. BREED ME

Welcome to the greatest show on Earth!

This is Dark Poeta.
  THIS IS A NIGHTMARE

Come one, cum all!
  NOT IN MY HAIR, PLEASE

To the nocturnal circus.
          DARK POETA

Vega Starlight

Vega Starlight

This is an ancient Chinese legend about two stars in the constellations Aquila and Lyra. In this legend, Altair and Vega are joined together in love but separated by the stars.

Altair lost his parents at a young age. After their deaths, his brothers decided to split their father's property. Altair, being the youngest, was left only with an old bull. When he was older, Altair separated himself from his brothers. With money he had saved from tending neighboring farms, he bought a small field and a few cows. With the aid of the old bull, he set to work building a farm of his own.

Late one evening, Altair sat down under an ancient oak tree and practiced a classic love melody on his flute. As he was playing, a white dove gracefully swooped down from the star-splattered sky. The dove fluttered around Altair's head. Startled and confused by this unnatural behavior, he swatted at the dove, but his hand missed. Having nearly been swatted out of the air, the dove landed at Altair's feet. The dove ruffled its feathers and transformed into a beautiful young woman.

Altair jumped. "Who are you?" he exclaimed.

"I am sorry to have startled you. My name is Vega, princess of the heavenly skies. I heard you playing and had to investigate. Who are you?"

Altair replied, "Princess Vega, my name is Altair. I am a lowly cow herder."

"Altair, the cow herder. You are a beautiful musician! Play the melody again."

So, Altair did. Every day for two months, Vega would descend from the heavens at sunrise and ascend once more, just before nightfall.

Vega, a heavenly being, was not allowed to interact with mortals.

One day, Vega's mother, the Lady of the Sky, got suspicious of Vega's whereabouts. The Lady sent a messenger to follow Vega. The messenger discovered that Vega was interacting with a mortal, and quickly reported back to the Lady of the Sky. She was so furious that she descended to Altair's field, found Vega, and dragged her back home.

Altair was stunned by what he had seen. He heard a voice calling his name in the distance and started running to find Vega. He came across not Vega, but his bull.

"Old bull, you speak? How? Did Vega give you some of her magic?" Altair asked.

"Yes. I know you love her, and she knows you love her. Get on my back. We will go to the heavens in search of Princess Vega," replied the bull.

Altair climbed on the bull's back, and they rocketed upwards.

The Lady of the Sky noticed the bull's scheme. To stop them, she used her magic to turn the sole pathway into a river (known today as the Heavenly River or Milky Way).

Altair came to the edge of the river and shared a final look with Vega. They both started weeping and wishing for a way to be together.

Vega's father, the Emperor of the Sky, saw their love and became sympathetic. The Emperor of the Sky created a wide bridge of magpies across the river so that Altair and Vega might one day reunite in immortal love.

Dancing in the dark.
No one can see my scars.
Please, don't touch me.

The Door Test

There is a rather infamous scene in the classic film "A Bronx Tale" where a young man asks a mafia boss for advice about dating a girl. The mafia boss tells the young man to give his date "The Door Test." Only then will he know if she is worth pursuing.

What is "The Door Test?" the young man queried.

The mafia boss explains, "You pull up to wherever she is. You get out of the car and lock the doors. You walk over to her, then you bring her over to the car. Take out the key, put it in the lock, and open the door for her. You let her get in, then you close the door for her. When you walk around the back of the car, you look through the rear window. If she doesn't reach over and lift up that button for you so you can get it, dump her. If she doesn't reach over and lift that button for you, it means she is selfish. You are only seeing the tip of the iceberg. You dump her. You dump her fast."

"The Door Test" is antiquated and likely not appropriate for twenty-first century dating, if for no other reason than most people do not have manual locks in their vehicles. However, the spirit and intent of the test still holds water in the 21st century.

The test can be used during the course of normal daily activities. You cover a shift for a coworker, but they say they are busy when you ask them to cover a shift for you. You prepare dinner for your partner, but they do not offer to clean the dishes. You text a friend to ask how their week is going, but they don't ask about your week. Someone says, "Nice to meet you," forgetting that you had lunch with them two weeks ago. You introduce yourself and give your name, but the other person does not offer their name.

These are examples of "failed door test," but there are an infinite number of similar scenarios. Simply put, these are selfish people who are showing you the tip of their narcissistic iceberg.

Allow me to pause and make a distinction here, dear reader. I am not suggesting that you keep a running tally every nicety, kindness, or self-sacrifice. Selfless words and actions are their own rewards, and it is not healthy to expect another person to validate or reciprocate. Charity and good deeds do not require validation or reciprocity. You do those things because it feels good - you do those things just to do them. Expectations are the great assassins of relationships. Relationships are give-and-take. Sometimes you have a bad day and need to take more from a relationship than you normally would. There is nothing wrong with leaning on a relationship when you need support. You do not have to reciprocate on every paltry favor. However, you must be prepared to give when you are finished taking.

What I am emphasizing with "The Door Test" is glaring, obvious, self-centered behavior. This is a relationship that lacks give-and-take balance. This is a relationship in which one person is unsatisfied, often chronically. One person brings their best to the table while the other feasts on the banquet and offers nothing in return.

"The Door Test" was a revolutionary concept for me. It has fundamentally changed the way I view all relationships. I hope that you can apply "The Door Test" to your own life to burn rotting bridges.

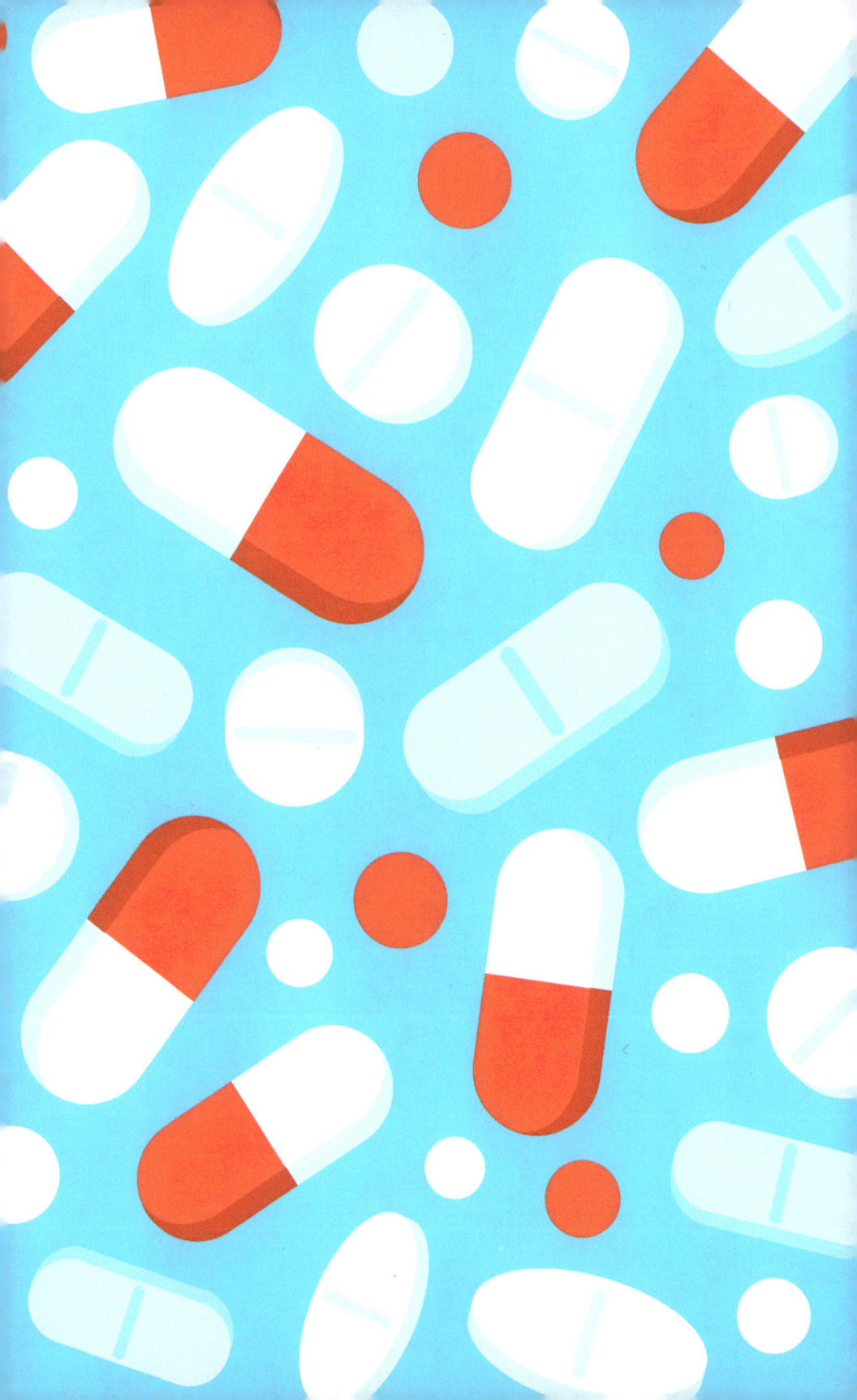

If you seek an escape from the harsh
realities of your life,

try a ~~mindless~~ **Feckless**

FANTASY

novel.

Or maybe pop one of those

PILLS

that you like so much.

I do not know why I am here,
but I tell you this:

Take me away.

In all that there is.
In everything.
From everything.

Do this tonight.
Tonight!
Do it tonight:

Go outside and look up.
Tell me I deserve to be here.
Tell me that you deserve to be here.

LIAR

You and I are nothing in the vastness of everything.

Humble yourself.
Adjust your morality.

And...

… REPENT

I hate

every moment

of my

Wretched

Reflection

MIRROR MIRROR

Mirror, Mirror
on the wall.
Who's the fairest
of them all?

If not for society's judgments,
I would not own a mirror.

The excruciating minutia
of vigilantly maintaining
my aging exterior
is taking a toll.

My mind is on auto-draft.
Pay the toll.
Pay the Boat Man.
What difference does it make to me at this point?

How strange to gaze at the body,
It blunts and dulls with time.
While the mind hones and sharpens,
More lethal by the day.

Good Days, Bad Days

How odd it is,
Good days are bad.
A good day for a poet,
Is the worst day for an observer.
A neutral observer,
Going through the motions.
Lacking emotions.
A good day for a poet,
Is an existential crisis.
A good day, a happy day -
Zero productivity.
The furnace is extinguished.
Fueled by hatred and rage,
The good day steals it all away.
Take it all away.
Sun shining, flowers blooming,
Birds chirping, summer looming.
Rape my mind,
And steal my drive.
Cap my pen.
Burn my page.
Give me depression.
Give me the feckless existence,
Anxiety - my weapon.
Another day,
Please say,
It will be bad.
Let me be far away.
Now.
You know.
Inside my mind.
This is what it feels like.

Cut me

Deep

43

Please.

Get me out of here.

Let me join you.

I can't do this on my own.

BURY ME

BESIDE

YOU

DON'T TELL ANYONE, OK?

Tiny fish, tiny bowl,
Sleazy wish, blackened soul.

Sunday is not for YELLOW

Tomorrow will be bad.
Yellow or plaid?
Yellow nor plaid.

We must mourn Monday...

WITH
BLOODY
RED

TRASH

I came upon a piece of trash in a parking lot.
Yellow lined pad paper, waylaid.
Used, burned, balled into cannon fodder.
Something compelled me to investigate this trash.

Lane,
It has been great
walking with you. I
wish all the luck
at your new job.
They are lucky
to have you.

(Someone) loves Lane.
Lane does not love (someone).
Lane tried to let (someone) down easy.
A new job.
An excuse to escape the relationship.
(Someone) was hurt but not deterred.
(Someone) left a note on Lane's car.
Lane left work for the last time from this building.
Lane found the note under the windshield wiper.
Just as Lane discarded the job in favor of a new one,
The love note was also discarded.
It was no longer a love note.
It became trash.
Another victim in the wake of Lane's selfish decisions.

(Someone) needs to move on.

Ringmaster's Note: Lane has failed "The Door Test."

~~VEGA'S~~

POETRY
is not an escape

POETRY
is hyper-focused reality

48

SARAH

Sarah.

WHICH ONE...?

None.

SIGH

Wash.
Rinse.
Repeat.

Ringmaster's Note: Sarah, Sarah, Sarah, Sarah, Sarah, Sarah, and Sarah have failed "The Door Test." *THIS ONE IS ON YOU*

ON YOUR KNEES

IF YOU PLEASE

51

Mourning Star

The fateful day did come when Heaven cleaved.
For Yahweh's throne, Lucifer sang reveille.
His sycophants rallied with arms to heed.
The Vain One's call to march on God, belayed.

Creator of the stars and moons, forsake.
My strength imbues this flock, a new council.
To build what Yahweh only dreamed to make.
On wings of death, I shall impale and kill.

Right hand of God shatters into bright light.
His scale of justice weighted towards Holy.
The sword of Michael falls upon the flock.
Through Heaven's clouds, the sky, the earth, a folly.

The Morning Star, Lucifer, fell to Hell.
Banished by Michael, a story God will tell.

I woke up this morning.
I felt ill.
I almost always feel ill these days.

Feeling ill puts me in a bad mood.
An eye for an eye.
I try my best, I really do.   **WALKING**

Autumn mornings are a special gift.
Calm, cool, foggy, cloudy.
The only sounds are the birds not strong enough to migrate.

There is a beautiful rainbow.
It pierces through a pink cotton ball cloud and hangs delicately
    in the foreboding atmosphere.
A rainbow just for me.   **AWAY**

I smile upwards and take solace in the rainbow.
I vow to be cheerful despite feeling ill.
I gaze at the rainbow and get lost in my thoughts.

Screaming.
Silence shatters.
Serene breaks.   **FROM**

The tea pot,
Destroys my three second relationship with the rainbow.
I am a professional at short term relationships.

Back to the mundane.
Back to the recovery.   **RAINBOWS**
Back to the grind.

Despite my best efforts and intentions,
My previous decisions always have a way of halting the
    present.
I want to stop walking away from rainbows.

INDIFFERENCE

Love me, eat me, leave me, hate me.
Emotional prison.
Flip a coin.
Call a side.
Heads.
~~Love~~ **HATE** and hate.
Two sides of the same coin.
Heads roll.
Emotional poison.
Escape your sentence.
Cheat your death.
The jailer's key is within reach.
The antidote drips-drips-drips intravenous.

SWALLOW EVERY DROP

Indifference is the only release.

LA PUTA

I'm in love with a girl.
She doesn't know my name. FORGOT
La flaka? La gorda!
Our humor, much the same.

Long blond hair.
Fat breasts.
And hips to match!
The things I would do if pressed.

Another single mom.
I'll destroy her life.
Or will she destroy mine?
Mutually assured strife.

No, this time I will hide.
Daydreaming of indivisible.
No, I learned my lesson last time.
It is better to remain invisible.

So I told myself,
But I never listen.
If she flirts with me again today, I'll ask her out.
Oh, how her lips glisten.

Oh my God, you are so handsome,
My name is Britney.
Thanks. Let's go on a date.
Sorry but I am taken.

I should have listened to myself.
I never listen.

Ringmaster's Note: Britney has failed "The Door Test."

ATTENTION!

Ladies and gentlemen!

In an unprecedented turn of events,
I have been alleviated of my torment.
La flaka, la puta, Britney,
Is not what she seems.

A friend did tell me,
La flaka is a banshee.
Bottom-feeder.
Queen of the Meager.

La flaka, su madre, y su novio.
Please do not text me the porno.
Incestuous threesome, money shot, full zoom.
Her kids asleep in the next room.

We dodged a bullet, dear audience! CLICK
Saved by the backstage jester! CLICK
— BOOM
Applause for the sideshow!

SUGAR PIE

I always liked your style.
Silent and remissive.

I miss You.

But you don't realize the evil of your actions.
Maybe W/we can be friends.
Strip away the intensity.

Why?

Because I don't trust you anymore.

I will try harder.

Then become weaker.
More desperate.

I cannot be less.
I cannot be worse.
I have reached the bottom of the well.
Wet and dank.
Touch me and see.

Then dig deeper.
Black and bleak.
Owned.
Controlled.
Nothing.

Nothing.

Say no more.
I need you to be more stable.
Do you understand?
Less impetus.

You don't even like me.

Nor does anyone else.

You will never leave Pixie.

Do you wish I had never met Pixie?

Does Pixie know that W/we still talk?

Do you wish I had never met Pixie?

I don't want to be a secret anymore.

Do you wish I had never met Pixie?

I wish only for Your happiness.

Goodbye.

Why are You on the floor? LIAR

Ringmaster's Note: Sugar Pie has failed "The Door Test."

YOU WERE NEVER MY MISTRESS
JUST ANOTHER NARCISSIST
AT PIXIE'S FEET

CARTE BLANCHE

Would You like to start with an appetizer?

I will start with something fun that will thinly veil my psychosis.

An exciting choice! I always order that appetizer. And to drink?

Just wring your heart out. I'll lap the blood from the table.

Another excellent choice! Quite a refined palate You have, Mistress. And for Your entrée?

I will devour your finest happiness with a side of your most delicate sanity. Blue rare, slightly bloody. Knock the horns off your heart. You will not be needing horns with Me.

A popular choice which I am delighted to serve to the Mistress.

I will also require a doggy-bag so that I can share your misery with My friends and family.

I am happy to accommodate and self-deprecate. Shall I present the bill now?

The service was terrible. The food was damaged goods. Your heart was still beating and throbbing, for fucks sake. I ordered dead and obsequious. I'll not be paying the bill.

If You do not pay the bill, then the money will be deducted from my paycheck.

…and a piece of cake before you close the tab.

Yes, my Mistress.

I
AM
DEAD
INSIDE

A failed star

Imploding

Into an insufferable

BLACK
HOLE

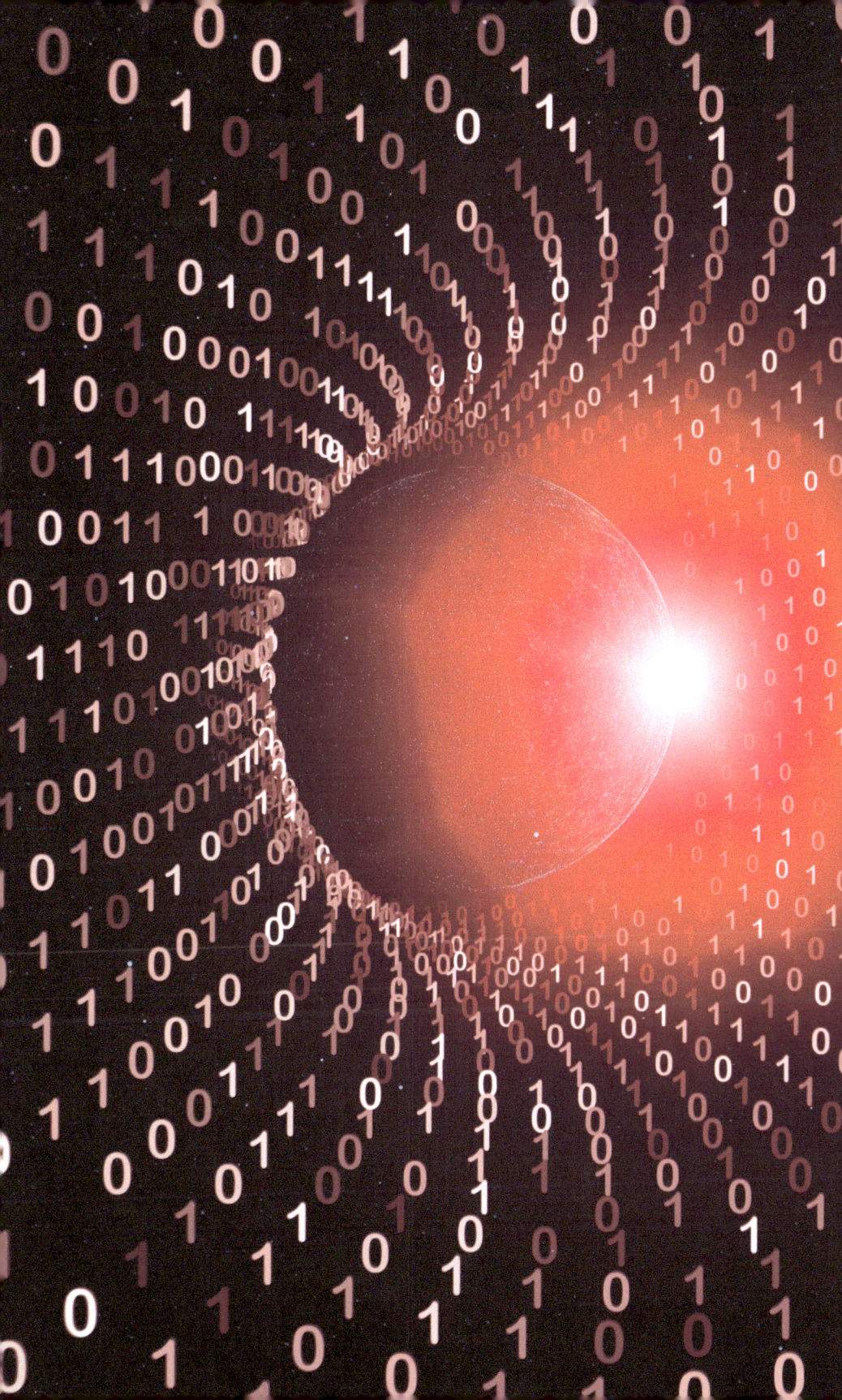

THE PATH NARROWS

A baby is born into a flowering meadow.
Gentle winds tease dancing leaves.
Bursting flowers put on a show.
Ignorant and unaware of the bereaved.

The path narrows.

Weaned from the breast.
Lacking words to express emotions.
Separation anxiety and unrest.
Medicines and potions.

The path narrows.

Walking is good.
Falling is bad.
Choosing a mood.
Why are you sad?

The path narrows.

First day of school.
Will they one day be President?
Don't be a fool.
Coddled and hesitant.

The path narrows.

Childhood diseases.
Vaccine injuries.
Chickenpox, pneumonia, measles.
Comply or be shunned from society.

Playground fights.
A stolen girlfriend.
Past your bedtime, turn out the lights.
A last desperate text, push send.

The path narrows.

Driver license.
Near miss, near miss.
Tensions heighten.
Mother's hiss.

The path narrows.

The invincible child.
Also known as young adult.
Zero consequences, be wild.
Choices have consequences, tumult.

The path narrows.

Time smothers.
Years strangle.
Friends are gone, can't find others.
Slave to society, career is a bangle.

The path narrows.

Blink once and you are old.
One thousand diseases.
Mortgage a cure, wherever medicines are sold!
The doctor will see you when she pleases.

The path narrows.

Blink twice and see a sickle.
Death has come, see the mice?
IV, heart monitor, stitches - life is fickle.
Hell is a broiler, smell the spice.

The path narrows.

World.
Road.
Tight rope.
Sickle blade.

The Rankle and File

The rankle and file.

Marching in line to their own beat.

Left.
Left.

Left, blight, left.

Twinkle

little

wonder

you are

so high

diamond

sky

I

Dear Vega,

I feel your:

expectations
frustrations
insecurities

Dear Black Orchid,

I feel your:

exhaustion
resignation
fear
lies you tell yourself
lies you tell me
confusion
searching
wondering
brooding
abandonment
anger
inability
inaction
camouflage
motherly instincts shatter
dependence upon the past
lovers, so many lovers
violence
indecisiveness, thinly veiled
bad decisions
broken spirit
desperation
respiration
delusion
tongue licking attention from a knife
failure

Ringmaster's Note: Black Orchid has failed "The Door Test."

CANCEL ME

Relationships do not come easily for me.
I work tirelessly at connection.
Days, weeks, months.
It drains me to the bone.
Working around the clock.
To make friends while suppressing my demons.
It is difficult work.
Back breaking labor.
Knuckles ground to the bone.
A war on two fronts.
Two theaters.
Two stages.
Two main characters.
Two fictions.
In an instant, a single moment.
Everything I have built vanishes.
One incident.
Months of being a feckless slug.
I conjure a spine and stand up for myself.
Other people stand up for themselves every day.
Yet they have many friends.
I stand up for myself once.
All the friendships go away.
I am told that I am a terrible person.
A terrible reputation.
No one has my back.
Because I stood up for myself.
Once.

People only like me when I am meaningless.

CABIN FEVER

There is nothing worse than not being able to do something.

Something.
Some thing.
Or anything, for that matter.
Snow falls wet and heavy.
The wind whips and lashes.
The door is frozen shut.
Entombed.
Snow drift.
Smoke rises from the fireplace.
Leaving the chimney.
Ripped into a wild torrent of snow devils.
Tiny tornadoes of snow climb and climb.
Then gone.
Snow blows sideways and erases the snow devils.
Life is good.
A hot shower.
Firewood stacked high.
The dog laid out on the hot hearth.
Plenty of food on the stove.
But the blizzard.
Stay inside.
Cuddle by the flames.
Heat of flames.
Heat of passion.
Heat of friction.

Skin on skin.
Fluid in fluid.
Read a book.
Sip a steaming coffee.
Sure, it is fun.
At first.
For a while.
But how many hours can this continue?
How many days could you endure?
Cabin fever.
Cabin fever?
No.
Not for me.
Cabin fever is for healthy people.
Sick people do not experience cabin fever.
People who have survived death do not get cabin fever.
Smash the door.
Break the seal.
Wake the dead.
Rise.
Go outside.
Feel the cold.
Am I still alive?
I feel the frigid cold.
The Winter Queen.
Her sword on my shoulder, knighted.
Prince of Cold.
I stand in the snow.

The blizzard tears at my face.
No jacket, no hat.
Just a shirt and my camera.
Soaking wet lens.
My hair twirls about.
Face flushing hot.
Wet snow pierces my skin.
One thousand Novocain injections.
A hospital bed or a blizzard?
What would you choose?
Give me the blizzard.
Give me the blizzard until I shiver, and ache, and hate, and love.
Give me the blizzard until it hurts so badly that I feel life.
So badly that I fear Death.
Feel it down to my bones.
His scythe slashes deep.
The cold and painful reality of no longer being in a hospital bed.
But somehow.
The hospital bed is colder.
More painful.
More deadly.
No.
Give me winter.
Give me entombed.

Cabin fever is for healthy people.

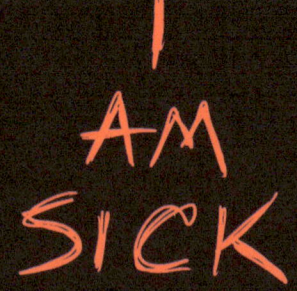

Mind the Hawk

The blackbirds hail from the west. Over the trees and into the field they pour. Cascading like the torrent of a storm swollen waterfall. The voluble blackbirds harmonize. Millions of songs and chirps each moment. In the same moment, millions of wings beat the air. A drumming so rapid that it is a singular hum. Black wings. Red wings. Brown wings. White wings. A stream of hungry vagabonds crashing down from the frigid winter sky. A fire hose of black noise. A black cloud of wings. Opaque. Black as spilled ink. Black as the night sky against clear, brilliant blue. Blackbirds fall upon the the freshly harvested fields. Corn to fill the bellies of the homeless. One bird alights, the next lands just a bit further, and the next just a bit further, and the next just a bit further. When the corn has been devoured, it is the first bird to alight who now finds themselves in the rear of the flock. It takes to the sky and moves to the front of the flock. It alights on unmolested corn. Then the next bird, who is now in the rear, follows the first and lands in front - the next just a bit further, and the next just a bit further. In this rolling, sequential leapfrogging, the blackbirds are a wave. A black wave as ominous as a tsunami. Countless and endless, rolling and cresting waves upon a cerulean sea. Cresting, crashing, cresting, crashing, cresting, crashing.

Stalking the blackbirds.
Sharp eyes, talons, death blow strike.
Nomad assassin.

RAINE

I hope you had a nice day. How are you doing?

Thanks.

Goodbye, Raine.

Ringmaster's Note: Raine has failed "The Door Test."

CRAZY

Crazy people lack credibility.
Crazy people are cut off -
From the demands and expectations
That made them crazy to begin with.

Naked. EXPOSED

They have nothing more to lose.
Free.

The most dangerous man,
Is the man with nothing to lose.

As I write this.
This very moment.
A moth is stuck.
Over and over it slams it face into the window.
I could save it.
Free it.
Release it into the bitter, unforgiving winter air.
If I free the moth, it will die immediately.
So, the moth stays inside.
More brain damage, more exhaustion.
When the sun goes down.
The moth will come to my desk.
Into the light, over and over.
It will be dead by morning.
Humanity has dominion over the animal kingdom.
We must do for them what they cannot do for themselves.
So, what is humane?
Death now or death tonight?
The pain will be the same.

Moth wants freedom.
Escape the glass.
But instant Death awaits outside.
His icy sickle etches the glass.
Inside is Death, too.
Inside the glass,
Death is warmer but slower.

The Tiniest Witch

I'm the tiniest witch in the whole coven. Most days, I'm stuck baking the slimiest treats in the oven. My sisters don't clean anything, not even the commode. It's so unfair. I want to explode! My hand-me-down wand is a brittle and weak. A twig that is suited for only the meek. Sometimes I pretend to be asleep in bed, but I sneak through the forest to a place that is dead. There is no grass, the leafless trees - so crass. Here lies a crude cabin, forbidden and evil. A house of darkness with corners never revealed. Inside, an old woman. Not a spinster. Something far more sinister! A witch not of proportion, nor of good fortune. My mom says that the old hag is a shaman of exploitation. The Coven Council shunned the old woman. They put her on trial, but she floated as if wooden. Killing fellow witches was her crime. Banished to an unknown forest, she does her time. I know the truth, she did nothing uncouth.

The old witch is my friend and treats me like a daughter, but I promised never to tell anyone. She teaches me powerful tricks and even gave me one of her warlock rings. She read my palm and said I will become the most powerful witch. I must obey her if I am to reach my destiny. The old witch taught me how to conjure a massive tiger, and I used it to imprison the entire Coven Council in cages. It is my job to monitor the prisoners and give them only enough sustenance to cling to life. The witch says that I must call her Queen. She says that my power is growing, but for now, I must focus on scrubbing the filthy floor. The Queen has been cruel to me and sometimes makes me sleep in a cage alongside the prisoners. I conjured a crow, a spell I learned in secret from the Queen's books. The crow slips through the cage bars. Find help. The next day, the most powerful warlock in the entire world arrested the Queen and rescued the prisoners. I don't have to clean anymore. Well, after I finish scrubbing burned witch from the floor.

Razor Blade Ritual

How justified would I be?
Staring into the mirror.
The daily ritual.
Shit, shower, shave.
Wash, rinse, repeat.
Every stroke of the razor.
I strip away myself.
One dead cell at a time.
I do what I am told.
I follow the rules.
I obey.
A slave for a corporate master.
How many times will I dream?
Of pressing the razor to my throat.
Pressing.
Harder. DO IT
How justified I would be.
Call out of work.

"BUT I'M TOO BLOODY"

Don't care.
Get here.
Come.
Now.

Yes, my Mistress!
I'll bark and whimper. **I WILL BLEED**
Right away, my Mistress! **ALL OVER YOUR**
Ok, Boss. **FEET**

How justified would I be?
How justified I would be.
If I ended this ritual.
Let me have one choice.
A last choice.
The only choice,
But a choice, nonetheless.
How justified I would be. **END IT**
Oh, to have control of something.

No.
You control nothing.
Get to work.

PERSEPHONE

Where am I?
I told you. I don't know.
How can you not know?
You don't know where we are. What makes you think that I do?
You brought me here. How can you not know where we are?
I brought you to this cave. I did not bring you to this place.
What place?
Again, I don't know.
You are lying.
What would I gain from lying to you?
What are you gaining from having me shackled and chained?
It's for your own good.
You keep saying that.
Because it is true.
You are lying.
Keep your voice down.
No.
Keep your voice down or I will silence it for you.
Where is the rest of my crew?
Crew?
I had a crew of twenty men aboard my ship. Tell me where they are.
I saw no ship. I saw no other men. You were lying unconscious on the beach.
Why shackle me? I mean you no threat.
It's for your own good.
As Her Majesty's knight and loyal servant, and as Captain of the Royal Gambit, I command that you release me this instant.
Titles bear no weight here. Keep your voice down.
Why keep me here? Why imprison me?
If I release you, then you will die.
I have to get off of this island.
How do you know this is an island?

We were disoriented during a storm. We spotted land but could barely make out the terrain through the fog and rain. Twice we navigated around the island in search of a suitable mooring to escape the storm, but we found nothing hospitable. The island was not on any of our charts. The wind violently shifted, and we smashed into the reef. We tried to release the rowboats, but it was chaos.

You are certain this is an island?

Were you not aware of that?

Then they couldn't have walked away.

They? Who is they? Walked where?

I haven't always been alone.

Did they leave the island? Is there a boat?

No one leaves this island.

What are you talking about? Where did they go?

They died.

You saw them die?

No.

Then how do you know they are dead?

They are dead.

Release me. I will explore the island. Maybe I can find a way to leave this place.

You will die. You need me.

Need you? I think you have gone mad.

Yes, you need me.

I think you have been alone too long. You're a lunatic.

My ship crashed here, just as yours did. Most of the crew survived. Our first night here, we found this cave, but some of the men refused to sit idle. They went out into the dark to search for water. They never returned.

But the rest of you survived?

For a while, but one by one, the crew went mad.

Mad is not the same thing as death. How did they all die?

The same way as the men who died the first night. Convinced that they could find a way home, they wandered out into the dark.

How do you know that they died? You didn't know this was an island until I told you. Maybe you were wrong about their deaths. Maybe they escaped.

They didn't.

You don't know that.

Trust me.

I don't.

If you go outside, you will die.

Let me make that decision on my own. You have no right to imprison me.

Look at this.

A book. So what?

A journal. The captain of my ship went mad and wandered into the dark. He left his logbook behind.

I don't understand.

Read the first page.

Captain's Log. October 12th, 1531. Departed from port this morning. Strong currents and trade winds. Will arrive ahead of schedule. Weather appears to be…

The date.

Pardon?

Read the date.

I don't understand you.

Your ship crashed yesterday. What was the date?

As I said, we were disoriented. November 15th, give or take a day.

And the year?

Are you serious?

The year.

1744, of course. You truly have gone mad.

Do you not see?

See?

The dates.

You were on a boat that set sail in 1531?

Yes.

Impossible.

I have been here a long time, but I did not realize that two centuries had passed.

Two hundred years? Maybe you are the one who went mad. Maybe the rest of your crew mates made it home and tell stories about the mad man who stayed behind.

I don't expect you to believe me, but you would be wise to listen to my warnings. Everything I have told you is reality.

Release me.
I will release you under conditions.
What conditions?
You will stay inside the cave tonight, and you will do exactly as I say. At dawn tomorrow, if you still want to leave, I will not stop you.
I agree.
So be it.
I should kill you.
That would be quite a reward for saving your life.
You saved no one. You're a liar.
I pull you from the beach. I revive you. I give you water and food. I release you under a gentleman's agreement. Still, I am called a liar?
What are these drawings?
I don't know.
You didn't make these drawings on the walls of the cave?
No.
Then who did?
Them, I would assume.
Them? What are you pointing at?
Look carefully into the back of the cave.
Is that a skull?
Several skulls.
Your shipmates?
The skeletons were here long before I.
How is that possible?
There is something wrong with this island. We are not meant to escape. This place is eternal.
There must be a way home. I will go search the island for supplies to build a raft.
You will do no such thing. You made an agreement to obey me.
Tonight, I shall. Tomorrow is a different story.
I will change your mind.
You will not.
Dusk has come. Darkness will soon fall. Follow. I must show you something.
What is there to show in the dark?
Keep your voice down. We have reached the cave entrance.

And who will hear me? Surely after two hundred years, you would be aware if other people lived on the island. There is no one.
Not people.
Pardon?
There are others, but they are not people.
Old fool. I am leaving. I rescind our agreement. There must be a way home.
No.
Unhand me immediately.
Sit down and be quiet. Just wait. I will change your mind.
What is that noise?
Them.
But you said there was no one else.
Not people, no.
But I hear them.
They are unnatural.
They are speaking.
Singing.
Yes, singing. How glorious it sounds.
Cover your ears.
The hymn of a Goddess.
Cover your ears. Do not listen.
They surely must be gorgeous. I must go look at them.
Come back inside the cave. We are going back to camp.
They call my name. They want to meet me!
You will die. Stop running! Come back!

COME TO ME

Come to me
And tell me
Whisper in my ear
Flick your tongue
Inside me
Tell me
Everything
You fear

After the Snow

Most people enjoy snow.
In small doses, at least.
Winter is my favorite season.
Snow falling outside the window.

But snow is veiled.
Snow hides the desperation of winter.
Or perhaps it is my own desperation which hides.
Or doesn't hide at all - staring out the window.

The preparation.
Water bottles, medical supplies.
Firewood, dog food.
Groceries, batteries.

All day.
Cooking.
Cleaning.
Tending fire.

I must be vigilant.
Must stay ahead of the crisis.
A desperate, lonely crisis.
I am the crisis - staring out the window.

Snow hides its loneliness.
Behind a crisp blue sky.
Inviting, welcoming, cerulean.
A sky full of clouds, frigid and lonely.

When the storm is over.
And the sun has risen.
The bread has been baked.
The fire, extinguished.

What is left?
Ashes and anxiety.
After the snow.
The weather is irrelevant.

What remains makes life impossible.
Sheets of ice on closed roads.
Empty store shelves.
Businesses closed, schools closed.

The world is dead.
A beautiful day, but life is shackled.
After the storm.
Exhaustion, loneliness, anxiety, boredom, entombed.

I find myself blank.
Blankly staring out the window.
How long have I been standing here?
Questioning every decision?

I could go on a walk.
Get out of the house.
Out of my head.
But the world is dead.

Would walking a graveyard liven a dead mind?
How complicated this feeling.
My mind is crushed under the weight.
The weight of my pitiful house.

My mind drifts and bounces off the walls.
It criticizes and judges, myself and others.
There is no cure.
"You're the worst case I have seen in my 40 years of medicine."

I love winter, I love snow.
Apollo, burn away this ice and depression.
Your chariot has arrived.
Illusion - perhaps delusion.

Just a cabin fever ~~dream~~ NIGHTMARE at the window.

Hello, Tiffany. How are you today?

I'm not sure. I was just going where the day led, and it's been really fun.

If you had one sentence to say to the person you love most in the world before you die, what would you say?

I would tell them that I love them. Not really very original, but it's probably what I would do.

Good - honesty is imperative. What do you value above all else?

Happiness.

That is cheating. What makes you happiest?

Honestly, I don't know. I've been trying to figure that out lately.

Why do you get out of bed?

Only because of boredom. If I sat in bed all the time, I wouldn't really be doing more than existing. The only thing that makes me happy is trying new things.

Goodbye, Tiffany. Best wishes.

Ringmaster's Note: Tiffany has failed "The Door Test."

Bleed Inside

Bleed inside.
You will never see.
Maybe you will hear.
But only if I tell you.
Inside is red.
Raw.
Glowing hot.
Red hot coals.
Scorch all that there is.
Attack yourself.
Stab.
Slice.
Wound.
There is no cure.
For self-destruction.
Medicate yourself?
Please.
We both know that's not an option.
Medicate the inside.
To affect the outside?
Please.
Let us not be ignorant mouth-breathers.
Troglodytes.
Decisions.
Make me bleed inside.
There is only one savior.
Scalpel.
Gut me like a fish.
Loosen the drag.
Wear him out.

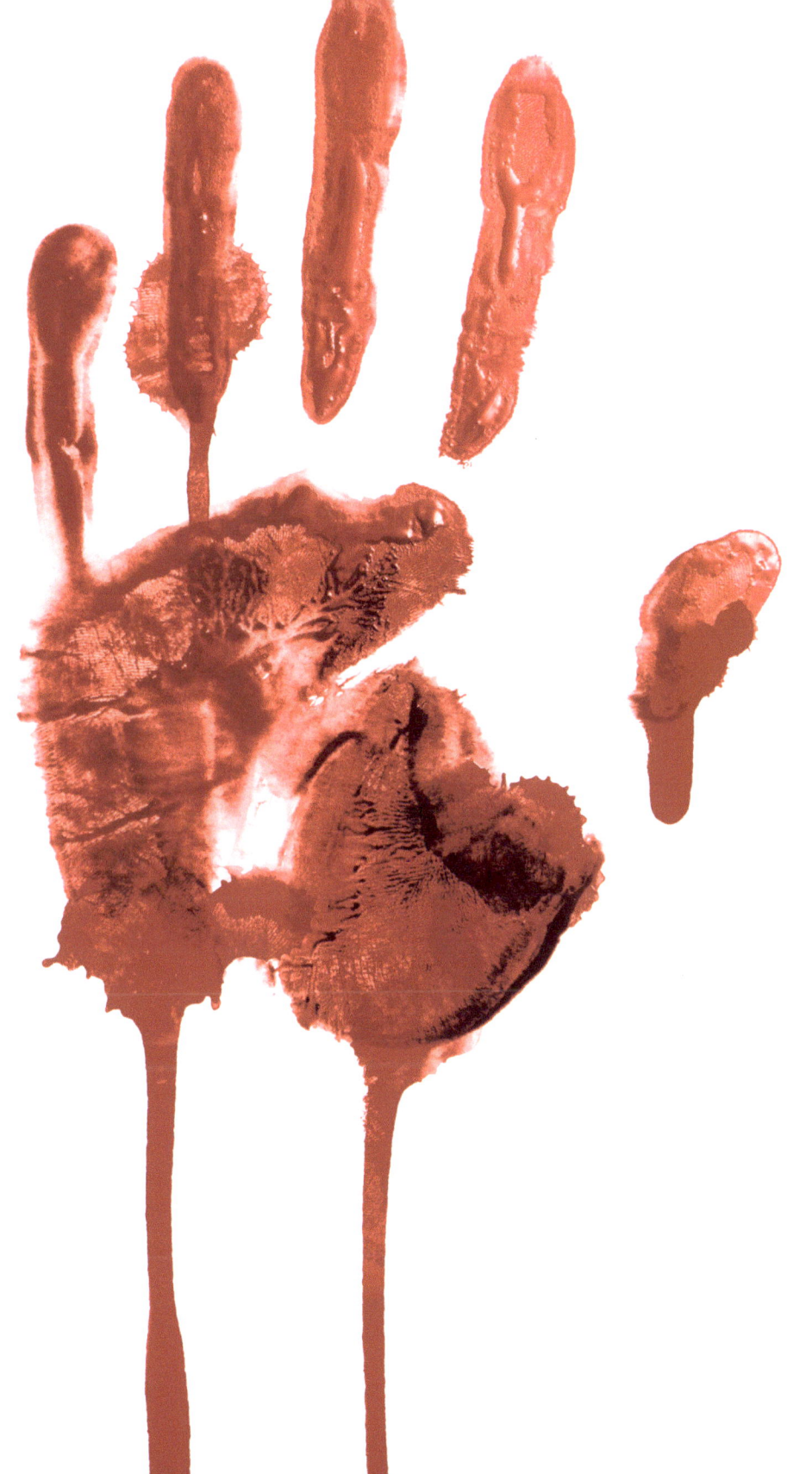

Tire his bones.
Drain his flesh.
Make him nothing.
Gaff his mind.
Stab his heart.
Make him nothing.
Make him bleed inside his mind.
Bandage me.
Hours and hours. *So many hours*
On a filthy hospital toilet.
Bandage his mind.
Head down, ass up.
Then fillet his guts.
No, you forgot his mind.
Epidural slips down his spine.
Sike.
It didn't slip at all.
But you don't believe me.
I felt everything.
You call me a liar. *It hurts*
No, I feel it.
You think everything is fine.
Nothing is fine.
But I survived.
Trust me.
I survived.
Even though I bleed inside.
I will survive you, too.
I will make you bleed outside.
Bleed with me.

LEX REX

Defend what is good.
Shield the righteous.
Guard the weak.
Banish the wretched.
Stand before the meek.
Pull back your hood.
Use not the gallows.
Look your guilt eye to eye.
Condemn yourself.
Drawn your sword.
Tip to your chest.
Fillet your breast.
Do as I say.
Not as I do.
Fall.
On.
Your.
Sword?
Die.
On.
This.
Hill.
Holy before ethics.
Break your face.
Upon my shield.
Sling your guts.
Across the battlefield.
The Morning Star means nothing.
False prophet.
False wannabe God.

Burn with your savior.
Michael, one handed.
Slice and dice your ethics.
Weigh and judge your actions.
Guilty.
Banished.
Go below.
The light of God.
The right hand of God.
Send you below.
Follow your savior.
You will never repent.
For there is no repentance.
You will never be God.
Silence.
We are not equals.
I repel your sins.
One handed.
Michael, right hand of God.
Retreat from me.
You have been extinguished.
You have been judged.
He's a loser.
She said.
Waves!
On your grave.
I stand.
The irony is so sweet.
You have been judged and found wanting.
You will never be us.

You will never be better than us.
We made you.
Goodbye.
Lex Rex.
Your actions matter.
Not.
You do not matter.
Lex Rex.
Your ethics mean nothing.
Protest this.
Click.
Click.

BOOM

SPLATTER

FORGET

Forget the ones,
Who have already forgotten you.
Wait, who were we talking about?
Oh, right.
Now I remember.
You.
We were talking about you.

Queen

Winter presses her assault.
How strange,
That ~~rain~~ could be colder than snow.
      Raine

REPROBATE

When we first started dating,
When things were fun.
You told me that men,
Your men,
Have a way of working themselves back into your life.
I didn't think much of it.
People say weird stuff when a relationship is new.
I thought you were just venting.
I loved you.
Gave you two years of my life.
The last of my healthy years.
Gave you everything I had.
You walked all over me,
Abused me,
Said the most terrible things about me.
To my face, to your child, to your friends and family.
I tried so many times to break up with you.
I could smell other men on you.
The way you rushed to the shower,
When I knocked on your front door.
I finally got away.
The same way their cum got away.
Rinsed down the drain.
Pushed away.
Down.
Into the blackness.
Their seed escaped.
Your lies escaped.
After two years, I finally escaped.
Escaped your gulag of despair.
But you came back.

Banging on the door, banging on the widows.
Threatening to call the police with stories you invented.
Leaving weird presents on my porch.
Getting your friends to drop you off at my house.
And you just stand there in my driveway.
No car, no sanity, no dignity.
A reprobate vagabond.
Where is your son?
Now I understand.
Now I see why men work their way back into your life.
You are a liar.
But not just to the world,
The biggest lies are reserved for yourself.
No one works their way back into your life.
You claw them back.
With hatred.
With sex.
With blackmail.
With threats.
With violence.
With vitriol.
With poisonous words.
With wet, lose, cream pie pussy.
Remember when you told your son,
That I only date you to cum inside your pussy.
I remember.
I'm sure he remembers, too.
With every weapon.
Your favorite insult?
"Nigger."
Your second favorite insult?
"Faggot."
Yes, I like to wear your cummy panties.
Yes, I like to wear your stained dresses.

Yes, I like to look cute while I rape you.
Rape you to make your foul mouth moan,
Instead of leeching hate.
Watch my bulge.
Watch it sway back and forth.
Under your dress that I wear.
Under your dirty panties I wear.
Pulled to the side, pulled up.
So what?
The only person you insult is yourself.
What a vulgar, sick person.
What a foul excuse for a human being.
I pity your child.
I pity the day he realizes that he hates you.
He already hates you,
He just hasn't realized it yet.
What a stain you are on my life.
On every life.
On every man who was ever lured inside of you.
They stain your panties.
You stain their souls.
You claw them back with every weapon,
Except for the tool that works the best.
Love.
Your son told me that he must be nice to me,
So that you can remain living in my house.
I never invited you to live in my house.
You just moved in.
I didn't even realize you had moved in.
All you had to do was love me.
But you can't.
You can't love anyone.
And it's our fault.
Your men.

It's our fault that you can't love?
No.
We tried to hard?
Cared too much?
Babysat your kid too much?
Attended too many of your family events?
Covered for your psychotic episodes?
Chaffered your DUI convicted, license-less, feckless ass too much?
I took your punches, absorbed your violence,
So the bartender wouldn't have to.
So my friends wouldn't have to.
My friends asked me to leave.
Because of you.
When you got kicked out of restaurants.
How embarrassing.
It didn't bother you one bit.
Oh, how embarrassed I was.
I am so embarrassed that I dated you.
I will never work my way back into your life.
No one does.
You gnaw your way back into ours.
Your men.
Like a termite on weak, rotten wood.
I gave you two years of my life.
My last good years.
When the sickness started,
You watched me crawl around.
Naked, crying, moaning, desperate for help.
Unable to dress myself.
Unable to wipe myself.
I crawled.
And you laughed.
I crawled on the cold, filthy floor.
And you mocked.

You invited men to my house.
While I couldn't get out of bed.
YOU INVITED MEN TO MY HOUSE.
Then had the audacity to claim that you invited them for my benefit.
Men I had literally never met in my life.
Invited yourself to live with me,
Told your child that this is his home now,
Invited men to my house.
While I crawled,
You laughed.
And you lied.
And you fucked.
And you stole.
And you destroyed.
You destroyed my books because you knew it would wound my heart.
Wound me deeper than your love could.
You knew that your love stood no chance against your violence.
I would rather die than crawl at the feet of a racist.
I hate you so much.
At the feet of a noxious, obnoxious, unconscious mother.
Blacked out.
Unconscious.
How many bottles of wine did you drink?
No, I didn't steal your wine.
You drank it all.
Drank so much that you forgot you drank it all.
Calling the police to report that I stole your wine?
Check the toilet.
You have been pissing wine for twelve hours.
I am so embarrassed that I loved you.
You made me doubt every aspect of myself.
Made me doubt every decision I ever made.
It has been six years since I last spoke to you,
And I am still single.

I am scared to go on a date,
Because you made me doubt that I can pick a loving partner.
You make me doubt my ability to judge
    a good person from an evil person.
I am single because of you.
You ruined my mind.
But I can say this about myself:
I have endured your words and violence,
I have resisted your pussy and sex.
You will never false-flag your way back into my life.

I will never be manipulated by you again.

Ringmaster's Note: Brandy cheated "The Door Test."

I Hate Myself For Loving You

You Destroyed Me

I Am Dead Inside

Don't You Want To...?

Date a nice girl?
Get married?
Have kids?
Don't you want a nice life?
Don't you…
Don't you…
Don't you…

Yes.
Yes.
Yes.
Yes.
Yes.
Yes.
Let's grab a coffee.
Let's try a date.

Oh, I didn't mean me.
I'm waiting for the right guy.
I want the fairy tale.

Wash.
Rinse.
Repeat.
Sigh.

I am not a fairy tale

I am a nightmare

My silence is so

Reliable

Venus

Lucifer, the Morning Star.
Venus.
He rises.
A star amongst stars.
The brightest.
Only to fall.
The furthest.
The farthest.
Heretic.
His banishment.
His failure.
Public for all eternity.

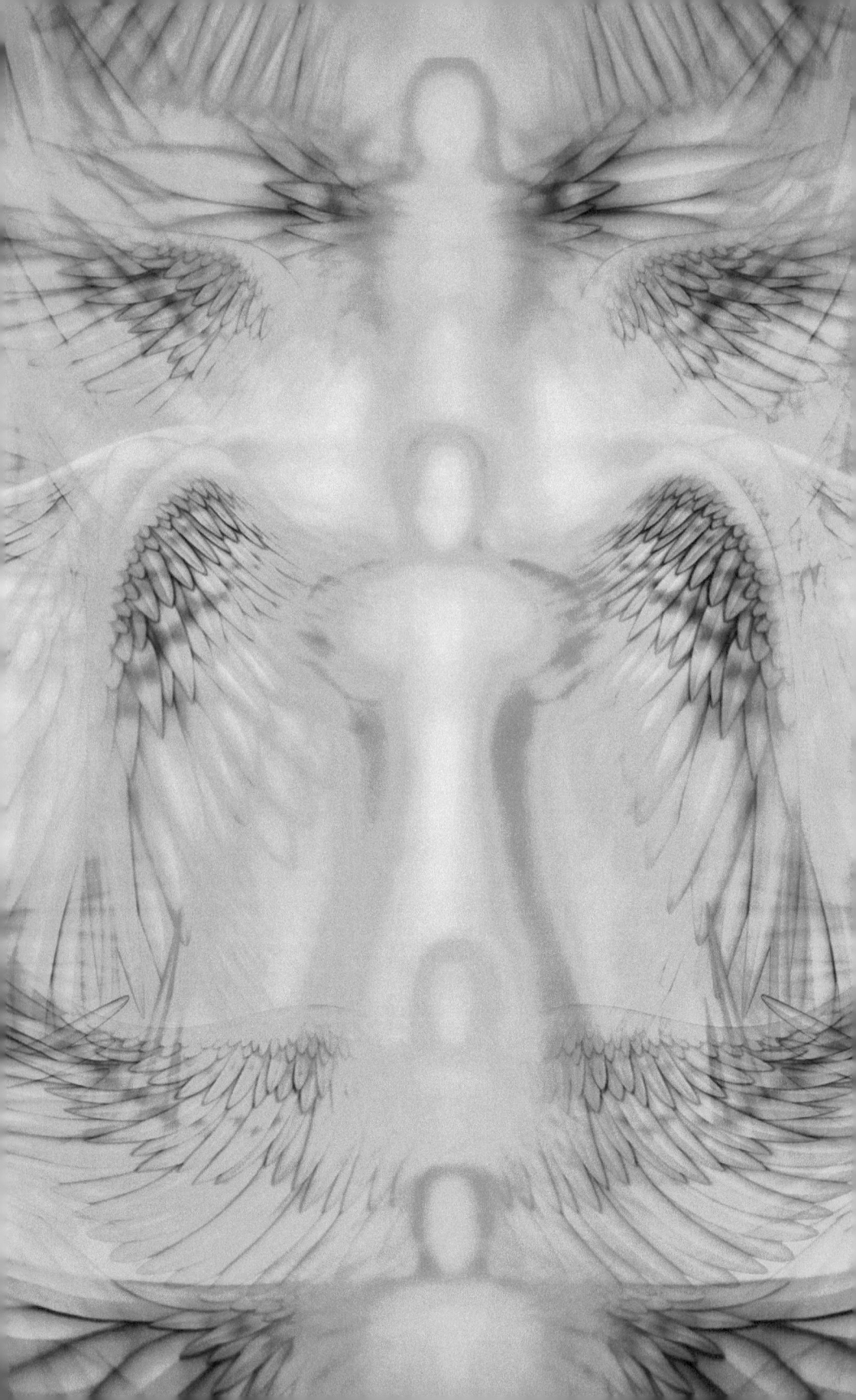

Winter Before Sunrise

Winter before sunrise is a unique and special gift.
It is difficult to find the words.
In truth, there are no words to describe the serenity and beauty.
Of winter before sunrise.
The stars are at their brightest.
White hot and sharp.
The owls are loud.
Their hooting and screeching,
An odd blend of love and aggression.
The coyotes howl.
Horny and bloodthirsty.
Yips and barks,
Shatter the frozen air.
Slice through your sensibilities.
Oh, the air.
The piercing cold air.
Refreshing.
Refreshing but deadly.
If your mortality is ever in question,
Stand outside in winter before sunrise.
You will find out very quickly if you are still alive.
The frosty kiss of the Winter Queen.
The Winter Queen is Death.
If you can kiss her,
Then you are still alive.
After your embrace,
Come inside by the fire.

Warm your bones.
Throw another log on the coals.
Drowsy, defenseless, melting.
A cup of hot coffee.
See your breath?
Fire in the hearth, fire in the belly.
Go back outside.
A volcano on an island of ice.
Listen to the deer.
Frozen corn stalks crunch under their dainty hooves.
The silent become the trumpets.
No one escapes the cold.
Or are they animals unknown?
Something dangerous?
Hidden in the dark.
The darkest night is just before sunrise.
Rooster crows.
Fox licks his lips.
Yes, come outside.
Exit safety.
Enter the cold and black.
Sparks fly from the chimney.
Shooting stars against the dotted sky.
A fireworks show.
Fire works.
Independence and freedom.
Foundations of liberty and cold.

Cornerstones of winter before sunrise.
The setting moon,
Illuminates.
Shines her fading glimmer on the barn.
The trees.
The ground.
Oh, it is hunting hour.
Maximum aggression.
The owls stop hooting.
They fly overhead.
Silent and deadly.
Killing,
The small animals who are brave enough to scrounge before sunrise.
My, how the coyotes wind up.
Like the compressed and anxious spring of a music box.
But the killing must stop.
The Winter Queen needs her beauty rest.
And thus, look east.
Razor thin,
But it's there.
Hints of blue,
Brush strokes of delicate orange and pink.
Apollo rises.
His chariot blazes westward.
Another day unfolds.
Oh, never mind.
It's just Venus.
Satan, the Morning Star.

HOME

When I was ten, my family moved to a new house.
A beautiful house made entirely of brick.
My father designed and commissioned the house.
One of the first nights in the new house, I had a dream.
Perhaps the dream was spurred by heightened brain activity as a result of a new living environment.
The reason for the dream will be left to your judgment, dear reader.
I have always had vivid dreams.
My earliest memories are not memories at all.
My earliest memories are, in fact, dreams.
I mention this history of vivid dreams to highlight the especially dramatic and memorable nature of this particular dream.
A vivid dream amongst vivid dreams.
The next day, my family and I went to my uncle's property and rode dirt bikes all day.
Despite the excitement, I could only focus on the dream.
It scared me, haunted me, and confused me.
It utterly dominated my mind.
To this day, thirty years later, I still remember every second of the dream.

I was standing in a kitchen.
It was not a sophisticated kitchen.
It was a kitchen of simple and meager condition.
A farmhouse kitchen.
Above the sink, there was a window.
Not a particularly well-preserved window.
The window was single-paned.
The window was painted a deep red.
The paint was not fresh, but rather, quite aged.
Peeling, deep red paint.
The surrounding wall painted white.
The window's peeling paint revealed rotting wood.

I stood at the sink and gazed out of this red, rotting window.
The kitchen was at on the backside of the house.
The season was early winter.
And the red window overlooked a vast field.
The grass was still green, yet it was short.
Blunted by the cold but not yet dormant.
The sky was blue.
A cloudless cerulean.
Sharp and bright and clean and crisp.
The field sloped gently downward and away from the back of the house.
Elevation dropping just slightly.
At the bottom of the gentle slope, there lay a pond.
A shimmering mirror of blue, a perfect reflection of the sky.
Surrounding the pond was a palisade of stout trees.
Oak, some pine.
The leaves had fallen, but not so long ago.
Standing in the sad little kitchen, peering out of the wretched little red window.
I felt calm.
I felt happy.
I knew everything would be alright.
And yet…
I felt a weight.
A heaviness.
As if something unavoidable was coming.
Something ominous and foreboding.
And impending event.
A path I could not veer away from.

I now live in that house.
For years, I have lived in that house.
The house I saw so long ago.
The house that haunted me.
The house that confused me.

I look out of that window every day.
I see the field, the ice-cold blue sky, the pond, and the leafless trees.
The deep red.
The peeling.
The rot.
Like an old man.
Wrinkled, thin skin.
Peeling away.
Revealing deep red, oxygenated, coagulated.
Flesh and blood.
I painted.
Repainted.
Green over red.
Healed the wounds.
Sealed the rot.
Paid the surgeon.
But what is old is still old.
Bandages on broken bones.
Now the green peels and flakes.
The house is dying.
From the inside out.
Before, it was just the skin.
Now it is the bones.
Breaking.
Crunching.
Sinking.
Festering.
Withering.
Decaying.
Being eaten away by maggots.
A cancer on the inside.
A cancer of termites.
And leaking pipes.
And mold.

And rot.
And green.
Rotting green.
Maybe I should have chosen blue paint.

You be the judge, dear reader.
I make no assumptions or assertions about the dream or my current life.
I give you the facts.

Promise me that you will never paint your house

GREEN

Vile, Sickening

GREEN

PAPER TIGER

Shred My Clown Heart

Billet-Doux

How ignorant I was.
Always smiling, sweet, selfless, supportive.
Love was right in front of me.
Exceptional, now excruciating.
You were the one.

Ringmaster's Note: Vega has failed "The Door Test."

On Greatness...

I know something about you, not even having known you.
I know that you have greatness within your soul.
You have the ability to do things you cannot imagine.
You have talents and skills for which you have not yet reached.
Gaze into the mirror and admit to yourself that you have put forth your best effort.
Unless you attempt to do something beyond that which you have already mastered, you will never grow. Design a goal that will make you stretch.
What is it you desired in the past but decided could not be accomplished?
Whatever it is, revive the desire.
When you pursue a goal outside of your comfort zone, you will discover new talents and abilities.
If you continue to avoid pursuing your goals, you will commit spiritual suicide.

Alive but Dead Inside

You may as well be six feet under.

Remember this, dear reader:
Practice does not make perfect.
Practice makes improvement.
Perfection does not exist.
You can always better your best.

You have not yet done your best work.

CRUSH

Be nice to people.
You never know who might have a crush on you.
Or love you.
Maybe one day you will change your mind,
And come to love this person dearly.
But for now,
Do not make your last words negative.
Make it about love, not rejection.
Do not wound a person who went out on a limb for you.
You never know if the last thing you say to a person,
Is the last thing they know of you.
If you are not interested in someone romantically,
Let them down gently.
Sometimes, people go away.
Other times, they go away permanently.
Be kind to those who desire you,
Even if you do not feel the same.
When they are gone,
When they are dead.
If you make your final conversation about rejection.
For the rest of your days,
You will be suffocated by guilt.
Guilt about the way you treated someone who loved you.
And then died.
Without a single word in-between,
Rejection and death.
Not a single word.
No reconciliation.
No friendship.

Do Not Be Like Me

Dear reader, I implore you.
If you take nothing else away from this book,
Please remember this:
You will not always be young.
You will not always be beautiful.
You will not always be successful.
Let not these material things determine who you love.
Let not these material things determine how you reject.
Be kind.
Be gentle.
Everyone dies. **YOU WILL DIE**

How many times must I learn this lesson?

Ringmaster's Note: Vega has failed "The Door Test."

NO STRINGS

Walking through a graveyard.
An old graveyard.
But also new.
Tombstones.
Old and new.
Long forgotten under the hedges,
Here is what I found:
"No Strings."
The antithesis of remembrance.
A nameless stone.
Lonely.
Only.
"No Strings."
I wonder how many generations must pass before we are forgotten?
Hedges tangle and corrupt the only remaining record of life.
A loved person,
Even without strings,
Surely they would not be forgotten so quickly.
It is impossible to die in the manner which we most desire.
And the irony of "No Strings!"
A headstone, a plot, a beautiful cathedral.
These are not the final wishes of the destitute.
Can there truly be "No Strings?"
Between the life and death of a person,
With such an extravagant funeral?
Such an elaborate graveyard?
Death does not cut the strings of the wealthy.
If you want "No Strings,"
Give your money to the destitute.
Erase yourself.

Erase every word you ever wrote.
Every pen stroke.
Go away.
Far, far away.
Prepare the boat.
Sail away from port.
Far, far away.
Drown your sorrows.
Drown yourself in the ocean.
Faster, faster.
Deeper, deeper.
No concerns of food or water.
This is a one-way trip.
Give your money away.
Just go.
Far, far, far.
Sail away from memories.
Away from everyone you know.
Away from anyone who might remember you.
When you reach your watery grave,
your whirlpool of nothingness.
Jump, dear sailor.
Man overboard!
Feckless slug overboard.
Cut your strings.
Burn your bridges.
Empty your wallet.
"No Strings."
Perhaps Thetis will collect you.

Cold Bricks

Ice rains down,
The world glazes over.
Fire warms the hearth of my soul.
My thoughts drift to spring clover.
The night is darkest,
When light is lowest.
Awake in the cold,
The fire slowest.
The clover retreats,
Leaving a bleak depression.
Brown, dormant, crunchy, brittle.
Another therapist?
Another session?
Icicles slip,
Pierce the soil.
My heart is punctured,
Cold bricks and turmoil.

BIJOUX

What Happened?
Who knows?
Fate.
Together.
Apart.
Fate strikes.
Once, twice…thrice?
Our eyes met,
Our hearts met,
Yet we fell apart.
Why?
Who knows?
Watching, studying.
A jewel bound.
But not to me.
Unbound.
Leased?
Or owned?
By another.
Jealousy!
But why?
What difference does it make?
We fell apart.
Or…did we?
Yes, we fell apart.
Time passes.
So much time.
Are you happy?
My jewel, bijoux?
Who knows?

Did you think of me?
Wait, I have a better question.
Do you remember me?
I remember you.
Are such thoughts relevant?
Shock and awe.
Campaign to see a jewel with my own eyes.
Emerald.
Green.
Envy.
Jealousy.
You enter the room.
But time,
So much time.
And pain?
Are you in pain?
Do these things matter?
What is real?
Jealousy?
Who knows?
I know that you ignore me.
Risk.
Take the risk.
Talk to her.
Crown Jewel.
Talk to her.
Bijoux?
You laughed at me.
Laughed.
In my mind, nothing has changed.
In your mind, everything has changed.
Laughed.
Memories clash.
I wanted you closer,
Yet you felt pushed away.

We fell apart but…
Why?
Who knows?
Certainly, I do not.
Liar.
I am a liar.
I ended it.
This relationship fell apart because I ended it.
And now you laugh at me.
Your pain is palpable.
No, I misunderstood.
The pain is mine.
I misspoke.
A heart full of emotion.
Could I have a place?
Amongst such pain?
A place in my own heart?
There is no room in here.
Do such thoughts matter?
I can't get a thought in edge ways.
Do you remember me?
Who knows?
I surely do not.
Will we be friends?
Lovers?
Haters?
Nothing?
You laughed because we are nothing.
I made us nothing.
Nothing.
I am nothing.
And you laugh.
Will we be a team?
Hand in hand.
Repelling the Evils of the World.

Who knows?
I know.
Nothing.
Just laughter.
Secrets of the heart.
Growth.
Pain.
Growth and pain.
Just pain.
Growing pains.
Lonely.
Lonely but not alone.
Liar.
Alone.
Regression.
Progression?
Regression.
Remission.
Getting over me.
Who knows?
I no longer do.
Liar.
I know.
Nothing.
My Crown Jewel.
Bijoux.
What are you?
What am I?
What are we?
Lost in nothing.
Where are you?
Who knows?
Liar.
I know where you are.
Where you are not.

WHERE YOU ARE NOT

NOT WITH ME

I WISH YOU WOULD STOP LAUGHING

I knew she had issues.
I loved her anyways.

Wash, rinse, repeat.

The issues are mine

i'm so sorry

IMMORTAL

The greatest legacy of mankind?
Death.
War.
Disaster.
Why?
Because we chase immortality.
It cannot be avoided.
Deny not, dear reader.
You also seek immortality.
Not a ceasing heartbeat.
Living in the beating heart
Of those we leave behind.
Living in their minds.
To live in the minds of countless generations,
Whom we have no chance of saluting.
Moses or Shakespeare?
Joshua or Dante?
Who is Godliest?
Who is the most Immortal?
Immortality is not derived from money,
Fame,
Popularity,
Property,
Success,
Nor inheritance.
Is art immortal?
Art is subjective.
Art fades.

Trends,
Ideas,
Mediums,
Politics,
Anger,
Happiness,
Phases,
Beliefs,
Clicks,
And styles.
They come and go.
But ink is permanent.
The story of art is not a universal truth.
Immortality is not subjective.
Immortality is objective.
Here, let me hold your hand and show you,
The objectively universal truth of humanity:
Only the heart is immortal.
Beating or long buried,
It matters not.
A warrior's pulsing heart,
Spills blood upon the ground.
A fountain pen,
Spills ink upon the parchment.
Words bind humanity together.
Words are timeless.
Who is remembered?
Who is immortal?
The warrior or the scribe?
The pen,
Sword of the immortal heart.

~~Cinderella,~~ VEGA
Sweep the ashes.
Bring the sutures,
Stitch my slashes.

THE MATADOR

Surgical precision.
Piercing strikes.
The tip of the spear is not enough,
To deliver death.
Just as one feather cannot fly.
A legion of cuts,
Brings the bull to its knees.
Just as the ink in my heart.
A slave to the pen.
One thousand paper cuts,
A lover's glancing blows.
Passive aggressive bitch.
Blood and ink,
Spills and splatters.

DICHOTOMY

Hi.
Hello.

It's nice to meet you.
We have talked for countless hours in the past.

Oh, I vaguely recall.
Good to know that I was memorable.

My boyfriend couldn't come tonight.
What a lovely topic. Tell me more.

I'm not supposed to be talking to anyone.
Lucky me.

What do you like to do?
Fall for girls who couldn't care less.

Am I one of those?
Yep.

I don't think I am one of those.
You are.

We were not on the same page before.
So, you do remember dating me.

I wouldn't call it dating.
Oh?

I don't write people off quickly.
You forgot about me rather quickly.

Do you mind if I hug you?
Sure.

My boyfriend is a great guy. You would like him. We have known each other for nine years but only as of recent did we become serious. It has been great so far. I'm really happy. Actually, he bought me this dress. Do you like it? He is taking me shopping again tomorrow. He wants to find some lingerie outfits for me to wear next weekend. We are going on vacation and staying at an amazing resort. I know we haven't been dating long but I can't help to imagine us as married.
Nice monologue.

I just want to say that you look really handsome.
I'm flattered.

Could you excuse me for a moment?
That's fine.

Sorry to interrupt. I had a phone call.
Who was it?

It was my boyfriend. Why do you care who called?
It was an innocent question.

I like you, but I think this is not a healthy conversation.
You have been telling me for two years that you like me.

Two years?
Yes, we first met two years ago.

Oh well. Regardless, I don't like your aggressive criticism.
Aggressive criticism of what?

The things you say are criticisms.
That's news to me.

You should think about our conversation.
I'll get right on that.

You are rude. I'm going home. If you give me your number, I will call you when I get home.
You deleted my number. Imagine that.

May I ask you something?
Ask me anything.

Would you have preferred if I said nothing to you tonight?
I would prefer to be more. I like you and I want to be more. That is my preference.

Maybe we can get together tomorrow after my boyfriend leaves for work.
That's not what I meant, SLUT.

So easily Forgotten

Vega is Nothing...

... Worthless

White Silence

Like a fresh snowfall,
The blank page.
Soft, empty, undisturbed.
A faint crunch, a delicate rustle.
One step, one turn.
Inhale the clean air,
Infused with moldy musk.
Ancient ink,
Long turned acidic.
Come play!
But be warned, brave soul.
Neither snow nor the blank page,
Will forgive your trespasses.

BLACK NOISE

There is only darkness.
A vastness,
Devoid of light.
A blight,
Upon what is good.
A plague,
Upon what is virginal.
A blackness,
Upon what is white.
Sulfur stifles sinuses.
Sniffing scathing.
Scorching sky.
The Morning Star.
The screams are agonizing and relentless,
Dante's sins and sinners.
What is a music note upon a page?
Black checks white.
Mate.
White always falls to black.
Surrenders its silence
Surrenders in silence.
Unless it is torn.
Black is potential.
Black is noise.
Scream these words:
Ink shatters delicate parchment.
Like a champagne glass,
Resonating harmoniously in the chaos of symphony.
Silence is shattered.
Reverberating through the void of cavernous nothing.
Black pierces white.
The breath of one-thousand trumpets.

Born alone, die alone.
That's what *they* say. **ALONE**
They. Who are *they*?
I guess *they* would know.
And in-between, what?
I'll tell you what.
Alone.
They forget to tell you that part.
Between life and death,
Beginning and end.
There is only alone.
We must bind our own wounds.
Bandage our own cuts.
Splinter our own shattered bones.
Mend our own broken hearts.
Maybe *they* don't know,
They who say.
Start and stop alone.
They are never alone.
They fear being alone,
As *they* fear life and death.
They will never know *themselves*.

Fear surrounds *them* with:

family, spouses, friends, associates, offspring, pets, acquaintances, bosses, coworkers, neighbors, relatives, cousins, uncles, aunts, teachers, lovers, mothers, mistresses, studs, that mysterious other.

They know nothing of alone.
But *they* know fear.
Heal your own flaws.
Bleed not your worrisome heart.
There is glory and valiance in alone.

LILITH

Hi.
Busy.
How are You?
Busy.
Haven't heard from You in a while.
Busy.
Are You doing ok?
Family, work, boyfriends, friends.
When can I see You?
Maybe next week.
Hi.
Tired.
What have You been up to lately?
Other people.
Do You have plans this weekend?
Resting.
Can we talk?
Busy.
But it has been days.
Going to bed.
You don't have room in your life for me.
That's true. Other people are priority, but we can still talk occasionally.
Goodbye, Lilith.
No. You are wrong. You are emotionally immature, and you are a liar.
I'm sorry. You are right about everything. Please don't go away.
I will drown you in a small pool of tepid water in the back country until you become a walking zombie.
As You wish. I love You so much, my Mistress.
Hi.
Busy.
But it has been days. **I HATE YOU SO MUCH**
Going to bed.
You don't have room in your life for me.

WHY ?

Ask yourself:
Why do you write?

All writers have the same answer:
To be immortal.

In all that exists,
The unknown depths of the universe.
Only the pen is immortal.

I have always wanted to be famous.
Perhaps there is still time.

PRISONER

Infected soul doth rot a putrid green.
Dark side, vile side, indicted vanity.
A pedestal upon which sits my queen.
My fate is tied to toxic liberty.

From simple words, rising thunderheads brood.
Gashes, slashes, forlorn hemorrhaged heart.
Her innocent moves amp my rancid mood.
In flesh my buried fangs shall never part.

A fling then ring, wedding and honeymoon.
Maintain altitude, wing is doomed to stall.
Rank gulag chains I must escape from soon.
Desert the girl before her rage, the squall.

A life of strife, I surely guarantee.
A child and wife, this path is not for me.

BUT I LIKE BEING A PRISONER...

Lonely

There is a type of lonely,
Few of us know.
Those with conscience,
Understand such woes.

My loneliness is self-inflicted,
Left over when I mourn.
A thousand bolts of anger,
My mind - a raging storm.

My phone calls ignored,
All the empty promises.
Trust built then shattered,
Love our token nemesis.

Those of us with conscience,
Are lonely because we know.
We deserve better treatment,
From those we care for so.

Best Friend

What do you do when,
Your best friend does not care?
Around the circle we go again,
Down another flight of stairs.
How long should I maintain,
A one-sided friendship?
A sickly, straining frame,
Crushed beneath its weight.
This show has worn me down,
But I hide the pain as best I can.
Losing my best friend is not affecting me,
Liar - you can barely stand.
Holding on for the sake of others,
For the sake of fake.
No, I do not mean the friend.
The children, the family, the mutual friends.
How long must I pretend for these people?
There is only one way this can go,
Only one way I can grow.
I am the villain.
I am the one causing problems.
I am to blame.
It is the only logical solution.
A best friend would never be such,
A stain on glass like pollution.
Beautiful stained glass.
Smashed.
Right?
Right.

What do you do when,
Your best friend looks into your eyes.
Into your eyes and lies?
Tells you that they have made mistakes.
Tells you that they will change.
Tells you things will get better.
Tells you they love you.
And then nothing.
Nothing!
Return to the same old same old routine.
Have you ever felt tolerated?
Made to feel obscene?
Even when you cooperated?
A second-class citizen.
Marginalized.
Denizen of nothing.
Why?
Because success eludes you?
No.
Because success means different things to you.
True success is self-discovery.
Oh, but not for the best friend.
Success means nothing more than money,
Defined by overspend.
Soul, heart, passion, intellect, pursuits,
Music, art, dreams, literature, nature, faith.
They mean nothing to the narcissist.
They mean nothing to the best friend.
No calls.
No texts.
No emails.

Have you ever been delegated?
My best friend delegates.
You have made it clear that I am disliked,
Why further insult me with delegation?
Treating me like an obligation?
Like an employee?
I am not your employee.
There is nothing more insulting,
than being looked down upon by a best friend.
A best friend should be equal.
An equal relationship,
Bring something to the table.
He judges a person's worth,
By how much money they make.
Not by accomplishments or intellect,
I really must eject.
I am exhausted,
I cannot continue.
I no longer fear the consequences,
Of slicing though the sinew.
I shed the fake and the false.
I reject the status quo.
To hell with what people think.
I know the truth.
My best friend hides.
He hides himself.
But I know the truth.
Insecure, narcissistic, shallow, passionless, medicated.
Fake.
An empire built on medication and therapy.
A family built with amphetamines and secularism.

To my best friend:
I tried.
I wish you the best,
But I give up.
Goodbye.

SOPHIA

Do not bring old baggage to a new relationship.
That is common advice, right?
How much time is needed,
For old baggage to dissipate?
Dissolve into the day to day.
Just another lover.
Every lover is different, as they say.
Every relationship is different, as they say.
They.
Always they.
One day, I would like to have a chat with they.
They have some explaining to do.
But I digress.
Four years.
Perhaps five.
A brutal, abusive, scarring relationship.
Five years.
Do not misunderstand.
I do not proclaim that after five years,
A person must get over their pain.
No.
I simply mean that after five years,
Pain becomes manageable enough to love someone new.
Someone new.
How long we have waited for this day.
Yes, we.
I said we.
Why? I don't know.
Every mistake is a new me, an old me.
Every relationship.
Every failure.

So many me and we.
Broken, smashed, stuffed inside of me.
Someone new.
Sophia.
So fresh, so new, so supple, so ready.
Sophie, Soph, So,
Sophia Mamamia.
What beautiful children you could make.
Just a seed is all it would take.
One chance and a seed.
Locked, bound, leashed, chained, restricted,
In love with me forever.
One seed is all it would take.
Have you ever made nicknames
For a person who does not know that you exist?
Sophia Maria Magdalena Sarina Falina Halina Katrina
They say when a person likes you as more than a friend,
They find a way to be around you.
Even if you do not know each other.
Again, they.
We really must track down this they.
I made myself known to Sophia.
Spent time around her.
Her slender, straight fingers working the espresso machine.
I wake up to Sophia.
Every. Single. Day.
Not literally, of course.
But she does wake me up every day.
Not only with coffee,
But with smiles, teeth, kind words, swaying hair, bouncing steps.
Sophia's vibrancy is like a flower growing from mud.
The blackness, the bleakness, the pain of my life.
And somehow, Sophia manages to flourish in my heart.

Weeks of this pass.
Then,
She notices me.
Something changes.
Have you ever experienced this magic moment?
When someone who does not know you exist,
Does not know you breathe, lust, yearn, dream.
She noticed.
She did more than notice.
She engaged.
"Have a great day."
She wrote this message to me.
A pen and paper.
Wrote a message to me.
Do you have trophies on your wall?
Souvenirs on your mantle?
Magnets on your refrigerator?
Small reminders of happy moments.
I do, too.
"Have a great day."
A priceless artifact.
And it is an artifact.
Do you know why?
I think you know why.
It is an artifact because this is not a happy story.
There is no happy ending for a person filled with:
Pain, regret, murder, violence, guilt, doubt, loathing, grease, dirt.
Have you ever held something valuable?
Something so impossibly valuable?
And then it disappears?
Like walking along the beach.
A diamond amongst billions of grains of sand.
A diamond glistens in your eye.

Pick it from the sand, hold it, cherish it.
Before you can put the diamond away safely in your pocket,
A wave.
You forgot about the waves,
While you were enraptured by the diamond.
The wave of blackness.
Forgot about the ocean.
Swell after swell pounds you back into coherence.
The drunkenness of Sophia is washed away.
One wave at a time.
Deposited in the backwash,
Gulping for air,
Slashed by shells,
Rubbed raw by sand.
But I assure you, my friend.
Are you my friend?
Probably not.
If you were, I doubt you remain now.
But I digress.
Another wave smacks you.
Hard.
The diamond is gone.
You can scrounge around.
Swim in the surf.
Sift the sand.
But the diamond is gone.
We had a great conversation.
I was convinced that I had finally found my wife.
Gorgeous, youthful, vibrant, faithful, musical.
Did I mention that she plays piano and sings?
Please.
I will faint if I discuss her anymore.
You see, she is moving away in a week.

Moving away to pursue her dreams.
It is not the dream of a diamond to be possessed.
A diamond must be among its own.
A diamond must be passed along from one gracious hand to
 the next.
Glitter.
Shine.
Hope.
Future.
What I bring is death.
Death of the future.
Death of optimism.
Infatuation.
Jealousy.
Shadow.
Rank and dank and meek and reek.
Sophia has God in her heart.
Sophia soars with Michael at the Right Hand.
I pray that God sees the regret in my heart.
Judges me as more than the serpent of the Left.
I wish not to be with Samael.
Have I made a covenant with Samael?
Could we have been something?
Sophia in love with a lowly poet?
A poet darkly?
In time, I could have convinced her.
Manipulated her.
Like I have done so many times before.
Is a shattered diamond still a diamond?
Dust does not glimmer, shimmer, shine.
No.
A shattered diamond is no better than sand.
Sand through the sieve.

I will repent alone.
I will grovel alone.
Grovel, wallow, hollow,
In the hovel of my old baggage.
I would have a chat with they.
And tell they that five years was not enough.
The old baggage,
Around my neck.
Can a Master wear a collar?
Oh, yes.
The collar of regret.
A leash that is permanent.
Inescapable.
"Have a great day."
Have a great life.
Have a great life, Sophia.
I am glad that you saved yourself,
From becoming my wife.

BLANK SLATE

Hate it all.
Leave it all.
Start over fresh.
Tear down the mesh.

Release me!

Survived your wake.
My mistake.
You're a waste of time.
Get out of my mind.

Unchain me!

Everywhere I go.
Buried under snow.
People always hate.
A blank slate.

Erase me!

Erase everything.
A new spring.
Survive the winter.
Crush the sinners.

Debate me!

You are wrong.
Tongue, two pronged.
Evil.
Weasel.

Judge me!

I am not worthy.
Other worldly.
Abused with intensity.
You rape with propensity.

Deny me!

I am nothing.
You are everything.
Scales of justice?
I'll not resist.

Scald me!

Depth and texture.
Industrial confectioner.
Melt my mind.
Peel back the rind.

Censure me!

No, I will not give up.

Please put me back in my cage.

Finish

"Life is not a race."
A popular piece of advice.
The problem with this advice,
It is only one side of the coin.
I will submit that life is not a race in the following way:
Your life is not a race against society.
Your life is not a race against other people.
I absolutely will accept this as true.
"Life is not a race."
But here lies the issue, dear reader.
This advice applies objectively to comparisons.
"Life is not a race" becomes problematic when we examine the individual.
The individual,
Their merits,
Their dreams,
Their goals,
Their achievements,
Their accomplishments,
Their reputation,
Their attitude.
In terms of the individual,
Life is absolutely a race.
But who does the individual race against?
If not other people,
If not society.
Who is the opponent?
The opponent is Death.
Believe me when I tell you,
No human can outrun Death.
The individual race we run has only one winner.

Death.
Undefeated for all eternity.
The race of the individual is more of a treadmill.
And exercise of running in place.
Yes, this is a doomed race.
But fear not.
There is hope.
You cannot win the race against Death,
But you can give him one hell of a run for His money.
Don't pay the Boat Man just yet.
This is what you must do, dear reader:
You cannot alter your race with Death,
But you can start a new race.
A race against yourself.
Finish everything you start.
All of your work, your dreams, your family, and your desires.
Finish everything that makes you happy.
Get on that treadmill and sprint until you can't breathe.
Until your sweat drips from every pore.
Finish your races.
You cannot win against Death,
But you can win victories along the way for yourself.
On the home stretch,
Stuck in a hospital bed.
No one brings a laptop into the ICU.
No one finishes their dreams in the ICU.
Death wins.
Death finishes.
Do not wait.
Go.
Right now.
Death is catching up.
Finish what you started.

THE END

The reality of poetry,
Is that it is never complete.
A poem lives, breathes, and evolves.
Just as the poet does.
Poet and poetry live in tandem.
Symbiotic.
Melancholic.
Dichotic.
The poet is tortured by poetry,
And vice versa.
Until the poet dies.
When the poet dies,
The poetry is finished.
Finished, but never complete.
Poetry can always be improved.
A comma here, a word there.
In this vein,
I call it quits.
You are finished.
Dark Poeta, the nocturnal circus.
This is your death.
Not complete.
Never complete.
Until the day I die.
But dawn is coming.
Winter's assault is weakening.
The siege is failing.
I am tired.
The insanity must rest.
Nightmares are coming.

Thank you, dear reader.
Thank you for looking at my reflection,
And considering your own.
We will palaver again soon,
Fret not your troubled mind.
We shall meet again.
Palaver and discuss.
Whatever it is that comes next for us all.
Us.
The people who try.
Try to improve.
Try to heal.
Try to escape the cage.
Try to serve someone appreciative.
Try to better ourselves, those around us,
    and society as a whole.

I Love You, Dear Reader

I Miss You Already

www.ingramcontent.com/pod-product-compliance
Lightning Source LLC
Chambersburg PA
CBHW041153270426
R18201000001B/R182010PG43661CBX00001B/1